HOW TO QUIT YOUR 9 - 5 WITHOUT REGRET:

A Practical Guide for Those Who Want To Change Job, Switch Career, or Start A Business

© Copyright 2017
Suhaib Arogundade
ALL RIGHTS RESERVED

No portion of this book may be reproduced, stored in a retrieval system, or transmitted in any form or means – electronic, mechanical, photocopy, recording, scanning or other – except for brief quotation in reviews or articles, without prior written permission from the author.

Cover Design by: MrV Designs
Edited by: Hafiz Akinde - Founder, Freelancing Pro

Suhaib Arogundade

© Copyright 2017|www.facebook.com/groups/themillennialemployeescorner

Suhaib Arogundade

DEDICATION

This book is dedicated to Almighty Allah for His kindness in making me conceptualize the idea of sharing my thoughts via this book and bringing it to fruition.

© Copyright 2017|www.facebook.com/groups/themillennialemployeescorner

PRAISE FOR
HOW TO QUIT YOUR 9 - 5 WITHOUT REGRET

The book is an eye-opener. I would have quit my job based on my emotion, which would have led to fatal career mistakes and ultimately regret in life.

   - Engr. Ibukun Olaoluwa; Civil Engineer|Lagos, Nigeria

The book is short and precise. I had to read it over and over and it kept making sense. It will definitely assist me to make my quitting decision. One last word, the book does not contain any BS.

   - Abd'Ganiu Adeoso (ASG); Chemist|Lagos, Nigeria

How To Quit Your 9 - 5 Without Regret will assist you to prepare well and minimize the unforeseen problem that may arise when you quit your job.

   - Moshood Haruna; Animal Scientist|Oyo, Nigeria

Great book.

   - Steve Harris; CEO, EdgeEcution|Lagos, Nigeria

Great book. I honestly believe this is a good book to put out there.

   - Gbenga Totoyi; Founder, Myjobanswers Career Community (A Facebook Group)|Lagos, Nigeria

© Copyright 2017|www.facebook.com/groups/themillennialemployeescorner

All praises are due to ALLAH, the one who taught man the use of pen and granted him knowledge of what he (man) knew not. May HIS peace and blessing be upon Prophet Muhammad, the noblest of mankind.

As for what follows, it was very generous of you to share with people your experience on such an important matter - quitting a job. For me, the book came in time. I was planning to quit my job. As required, I performed the 2 rakat of istikhaarah prayer, then I was in search for the right person to discuss the issue with before taking a final decision (we have been ordered to seek advice from the right people). This was my situation when I read "**How to Quit Your 9-5 Without Regret**". *What an excellent guide it is!* Following the guides, I decided to pause and take my time to give answers to the questions provided in the book. And now, I can see things a bit clearer.

The book is unique. It presents the subject very clearly. Yes, it is because the writer did not just write but spoke from his rich experience. A very good part of the book -**How to Quit Your 9-5 Without Regret** is the chapter of gratitude. It is helpful in several stages: During the job (before quitting)- it helps.

It serves as a *secret motivation that manages stress* and keeps one from complaints. Rather, it helps one to focus on what need to be accomplished and how to go about it. And after leaving the job, it provides one with an answer to the question that may be asked about the previous job or question like 'how do you manage such and such (ugly) situations?'

After reading the book, I see myself as a Graduate Intern who has come to build experience and apply theory to a practical situation in my current job. I now have good justifications for leaving.

I think the book - **How to Quit Your 9-5 Without Regret** is more than a guide to quitting a job but a general guide for employees. It will help employees to know their worth/level and if keeping their job is the right path for them to achieve their life goals or if it is best to leave the job.

- Ahmed Tukur; Agriculturist|Abuja, Nigeria

How to Quit Your 9-5 Without Regret is the first book on employment that I have read that is short, concise, and readily understandable. It opened my mind to appreciating what I am doing at the moment in preparation for where I want to move on to in my career sojourn.

- Abd'Gafar Bamigbade; Microbiologist|Oyo, Nigeria

Reading this book - **How to Quit Your 9-5 Without Regret** assisted me in gaining clarity on what I should do regarding my skills. I now understand that passion alone is not enough. Indeed, the book is an eye-opener. Thank you so much for this book Suhaib.

- Hajarah Lasisi; Physiotherapist|Lagos, Nigeria

© Copyright 2017|www.facebook.com/groups/themillennialemployeescorner

AUTHOR'S NOTE

I wrote this concise book to show you the simple steps to adopt in thinking through your decision to quit your job. Whether your decision to quit your present job was informed by the thoughts of a job change, a career switch, or a transition to start your own business, whatever it is that has stimulated that thought or desire to quit in you, you will find this book a great companion that will assist you to jump ship.

I have approached each chapter from the angle of *"quitting your job and setting yourself up for success in your next move"* which happens to be your sole purpose of reading the book in the first place.

Nobody wants to read a book that will take another research before understanding the concept or message the book is trying to pass across. Hence, I have brought this understanding into putting together this piece you are holding. The contents have been simplified but are thought-provoking.

My aim is to ensure that you read, digest, and finish this book once you pick it up. I would be more than glad if you could finish this book before going to bed.

PREAMBLE

Quitting your job is not something to treat with kid gloves especially in today's world where millions of people are unemployed and, yet, millions of people are still graduating from college every year to join the job market. If you already have a job with a steady paycheck, I bet you would think twice before quitting such job.

However, the process of thinking through does not have to be a traumatic experience. There should be some foolproof methods to assist you to know when you are ready and what you should arm yourself with. This will help to make the transition process an easy one.

"How to Quit Your 9 - 5 Without Regret" is that foolproof resource you typically need. I will show you what you need to start doing now that will give you clarity on your decision and make you enjoy the process all the way.

I have adopted an unconventional approach to teaching you what you need to consider in quitting your job. Thus, you might find some of the content unusual to the topic of discussion. But I can assure you that if you practice what the book teaches, you will make a success of the process and your final decision.

© Copyright 2017|www.facebook.com/groups/themillennialemployeescorner

CONTENTS

Chapter 1:   Practice Gratitude

Chapter 2:   Develop the right Philosophy

Chapter 3:   Work on your Attitude

Chapter 4:   Have the right Discipline

Chapter 5:   Audit your present Knowledge and Skill-set

Chapter 6:   Audit your Network

Chapter 7:   Create a Plan

Chapter 8:   Practice your Craft

Bonus Chapters

Chapter 9:   Find your Purpose

Chapter 10:   Build a Deep Pocket

Chapter 11:   Quit with your head, not your emotions

© Copyright 2017|www.facebook.com/groups/themillennialemployeescorner

Suhaib Arogundade

Chapter 1

Practice Gratitude

"And (remember) when your Lord proclaimed: If you are grateful, I will surely increase you in favor..."
- Q14 vs 7

Dollar for your thought

Imagine you giving a gift or rendering assistance to someone and the person does not show any sign of gratefulness. Imagine how you will feel for a moment.

On the flip side, imagine that person showing a deep sense of appreciation and thanking you sincerely for the gift or help you had rendered. *Imagine that now!*
How does that make you feel?

As human beings, we savor being appreciated and it releases an emotion of gratification within us which makes us feel happy and, in some cases, excited. This is what practicing gratitude does.

If you take an account of your present situation and think about the little things you have been able to accomplish by virtue of the current job you have, you will discover that there is something to be grateful for.

Even if you have not accomplished anything noteworthy, the fact that you have that job which can atleast feed you is enough. There are those who would gladly accept that job no matter how meager the salary is; just to survive.

Now, think about that for a moment.

© Copyright 2017|www.facebook.com/groups/themillennialemployeescorner

What happens to us most times is that we are lost in our wants and we fail to see the benefits we enjoy by virtue of what we have at the moment. The day I started to see my current employment as a blessing, and started practicing gratitude, was when I began to experience internal peace. I started working more productively and exploring new learning opportunities to get better at the job.

There is something very significant about being grateful for what you have. It enlarges your heart and frees you of worry which will then open the door for more opportunities.

Do this and thank me later.

Action: Kindly let me help you practice gratitude. Shall we? Let's do this!

Before you continue reading, I want you to take a mental journey. Think about the good things that have happened in your life since you got the job you are doing presently.

Have you done that?

Write them down.

_____
_____
_____

Now, show gratitude for each of them.

And as you do this, remember what John F. Kennedy said - *"As we express our gratitude, we must never forget that* the highest appreciation is not to utter words, but to live by them."

If you cannot think of anything wonderful that has happened to you since you have been employed, just be grateful for having something to do at the moment.

Chapter 2

Develop the Right Philosophy

"Philosophy is the major determining factor in how your life works out."
- Jim Rohn

Dollar for your thought

Take a second or two to think about why you are doing your current job.

Why am I doing this job?

Why do I want to quit now?

Caution: Don't practice the blame game here or start looking for some excuses to justify why you want to quit. The reason has to be about you alone.

Thinking about the reasons you took the job you are doing will help you realize what attracted you towards the job in the first place and why you are losing steam now, to the point of wanting to quit. This is quite important to understand the driving force behind your decision. It will equally assist you to form the right perspective before proceeding into your next engagement; be it another job, career path, or starting your own business.

You have to understand that having the right philosophy is crucial to attaining a desirable outcome in whatever choice you make when you finally quit. This assisted me when I left my first job. However, I would say that it was a half-baked decision as I failed to critically assess the whole situation and also lacked some of the other factors needed to achieve utmost success.

And that is why you are reading this book - so that you can think through the whole process and know the other factors required to get you to where you want to be which is fulfillment in whatever you choose to do after quitting. Although this does not mean that you would not encounter some bumps along the way but it will minimize it and also, you will be prepared to tackle it.

Action: Would you like me to assist you in forming your own philosophy? It will be fun. Follow me!

a.   Think!

Oh no! Thinking again?! I know, thinking can be boring but hey that's why I am here to guide you. If you have gotten a dollar for your thought in the beginning of the chapter, just transfer the response here.

_____
_____
_____
_____
_____

Now give a response to this also:

Who are you, that is, what makes you YOU?

_____
_____
_____
_____

© Copyright 2017|www.facebook.com/groups/themillennialemployeescorner

b.   Use your mind

Here, I want you to declutter your mind.

What are the things you constantly focus your mind on, whether related to your job or otherwise? Write down everything that comes to your mind.

_____
_____
_____
_____

Can you see any trend?

c.   Process ideas

Use the response in (a) and (b) above to come up with a philosophy that can guide you. Don't worry if you cannot come up with one now. Give it some time; it took me a lot of time to come up with one myself. You need to understand yourself to have an operating philosophy.

Chapter 3

Work on your Attitude

"Attitude is Everything."
  - Jeff Keller

Dollar for your thought

Can you remember one event that you approached with an awesome attitude and what the outcome was?

Having the right attitude towards things including the job you want to leave is very necessary for your next escapade. Whether you want to change your job because of a better or mouth-watering offer that you just got, switch your career or start your own business, you must never treat your present job with disdain. Rather, cherish it for what it is at the moment.

Overlook the naughty colleagues or annoying boss or the crazy workload and just approach your role with all the feeling of joy and excitement you can muster. You want to ensure that you are moving on with the right frame of mind which, I bet you, is very important for your next career journey.

In fact, this kind of approach will let you discover some learning opportunities that you can quickly take advantage of before calling it quit with your present job. This was how I learnt to be good at Microsoft PowerPoint while interning and this actually paid some of my bills throughout my period of hustle.

The way you treat your current job is the way you will end up treating the next role you end up taking. It's only a matter of time. Ideally, you should start developing the right attitude now that you are still nurturing the thoughts or planning to leave your job.

Action: Now, let's get the positive attitude adrenaline pumping!

Write down what makes you excited about your job.

_____
_____
_____
_____

I want you to focus on that and preoccupy your mind with it every time you get to work while doing your job or running some errands.

CHAPTER 4

Have the Right Discipline

"Discipline is the bridge between goals and accomplishment."
- Jim Rohn

"Without discipline, there is no life at all."
- Katharine Hepburn

Dollar for your thought

Kindly think of a particular routine that you engage in regularly? What has made that routine stick up till now?

Why do we study the lives of successful people?

Your guess is as good as mine.

You answer with such an aura of confidence... "Because we want to learn how to be successful, of course"!

That's a great response, buddy.

Now, do you know what separates them from the wannabe "Successful People"?

It is the little acts of discipline which they practice daily that accumulates over a period of time.

That sounds like a ground-breaking discovery from me right?! Hahahahaha

You need to set-up yourself for the journey you are about to start. Changing a job or career or transitioning into starting your own business comes with its own challenges no matter how well prepared you are.

Once you make the switch, you will soon discover that you need some form of system in settling into your new role. This is especially important during your job search period (if you have not gotten one before quitting your previous job) or if you are starting your own business.

Discipline births more discipline and more discipline and the cycle goes on. If you are disciplined in one area of your life, it will affect the other parts positively and you slowly start to become disciplined in those other parts with conscious effort on your part, of course.

Let me share a short story of how I have used little acts of discipline to enhance my life and my job. And that is how this book you are reading also came to life.

It started when I was preparing for a professional examination. I practiced utilizing my mornings to prepare for the exam and shunned sleeping after the morning prayers. After the exams, I told myself, "can't I utilize my mornings to walk some couple of miles around the blocks since I have plans to raise my fitness level?" And that was how I started. I did this for a day or two, just walking for about 20minutes.

Again, I thought I should revive my reading habit since I had stopped self-development for a while. Then, on day three, I walked for about two hours and I incorporated listening to an audiobook during the morning walk. Needless to say what I have achieved so far. It was one of the audiobooks I listened to that eventually helped to enhance my relationship with my colleagues and clients. Since then, there has been no turning back.

The story is still lengthy but for the purpose of this book, this bit should help. I hope you can see how one small act of discipline metamorphosed into others and enhanced my personal life and career. It is that sort of system I am talking about which will form your routine.

It works.

How do I know?

Because I have studied many successful people and it worked for them and it is working for me.

So I challenge you to start focusing on discipline today and watch yourself soar high. It could be by reading a page a day from that book you have been dying to read or start module one of that online course you have enrolled in to enhance your competitive advantage in your career or start a walk around the block for fitness purpose.

Anything it is, just start.

Starting is the hardest part. Once you begin - and with the firm knowledge of the expected outcome you so desire – you will never think of stopping. And that sets you on the path of birthing a new YOU.

Action: Let's commence the process of birthing a new YOU. It can't be simpler than this! (Smiles)

Write down one act of discipline you have always wanted to start and state how you intend to begin.

_____
_____
_____
_____
_____

© Copyright 2017|www.facebook.com/groups/themillennialemployeescorner

If you do not have one, don't sweat it. I will help you. I'm a nice guy.

Do you have someone you admire a lot and would like to be like?

I know you do. And if you don't, look around for one. (Smiles)

Then, find out what he/she does that makes him/her standout. Pick one simple act of discipline from this person that you can begin immediately and you will grow into inculcating more discipline by yourself as time goes on. The goal is to get you started immediately.

CHAPTER 5

Audit Your Knowledge and Skillset

"No man's knowledge can go beyond his experience."
- John Locke

"You must know all there is to know in your particular field and keep on the alert for new knowledge. The least difference in knowledge between you and another man may spell his success and your failure."
- Henry Ford

Dollar for your thought

Reflect on a time when you applied your knowledge about something to solve a particular problem. How did you feel being the smartest person in the room?

The elated feeling that comes from completing a task when others have been trying to find a solution but all to no avail is beyond comprehension. There is this internal satisfaction and you start feeling like your head is touching the ceiling.

Have you ever felt such before?

Your response might be... absolutely!

This is what having adequate knowledge and corresponding skills can do for you. Knowledge is not about the schools you attended or the degree you have acquired. It is about the experience you have acquired over time and the skills you have mastered that you can apply effectively without difficulty.

Bankole Williams; Convener of Live Your Dreams Africa, once shared the story of how he had to go work for a firm for a lesser salary just to acquire the skills he needed in the career he wanted to switch to.

Having a clear picture of what you want to do next after leaving your job will assist you to know the exact knowledge and skillset you would require to forge ahead without getting stuck halfway through your journey.

This was what assisted Bankole Williams to identify the firm to join in order to acquire the knowledge he required. He was clear on what he wanted to do next after leaving his banking job then.

In fact, Wale Tejumade (Convener, Lofty Height Conference) had to go work for a firm without pay for a year just to acquire the necessary knowledge and skillset he needed for his planned career switch.

To understand if the knowledge or set of skills you presently possess are adequate for your next career journey, kindly consider these questions:

What am I naturally good at?

Is it sufficient for what I intend to do when I leave my current job?

What are the things I do on a daily basis in my current role and job?

What would I be doing next; would I be applying the same knowledge or do I need to fine-tune it or acquire some new knowledge?

© Copyright 2017|www.facebook.com/groups/themillennialemployeescorner

You should write down your responses to the above questions. Once you have done this, you should have an idea whether you need to acquire additional knowledge and skills when you jump ship or not.

More often than not, you would need some sort of improvements in certain areas of your knowledge especially if you are changing your career or starting your own business. For ideas on how you can improve your knowledge and skillset, check the appendix section.

Action:

If you are changing your job;

Get one person you can talk to in the next job you are planning to move to and ask about what the roles you are eyeing entails. You could also enquire about what working in their company looks like. This will let you know if you need to acquire some sort of skills to fit into the company assuming your knowledge is adequate for the role itself.

If you are changing your career;

Identify one person you can talk to in the new career you want to move to so as to know the additional knowledge you should be acquiring immediately.

If you are starting your own business;

Read and learn all you can about the business before jumping ship. Also, look for one person already doing what you want to do or something similar and ask questions about what starting that business entails.

When you do this, I can assure you that you will get to discover the other skills you would need in your transitioning journey. Once you have identified them, you should begin the process of acquiring the knowledge or skills immediately.

Chapter 6

Audit your Network

"Your network determines your net worth."
- Anonymous

Dollar for your thought

Can you remember a time when you were in dire need of something or when you desperately needed to get something done?

Who did you turn to?

Someone you knew was capable.

It is no more news that people are our new goldmine.

With the right set of people around you, you will have access to an unlimited number of resources and opportunities that can assist you in making the change from your current job to your newly chosen path. But you have to be able to effectively utilize your network and these opportunities to get the desirable outcome.

A quick example is your reading this book. If you practice the guide this book provides, then you have successfully utilized your network and the opportunity it provides because I am already part of your network since you have read my book.

Surprised?! It's as simple as that.

Building your network is very easy. Your only have to work on improving your interpersonal relationship.

PS: Check the appendix for various sources of network in case you need ideas on how to build your network.

Your current colleagues or employer also form part of your network. Hence, you need to maintain a good relationship with them as you might need them for reference purpose or even as customers or clients in the nearest future.

Uju Matilda Dawodu (Author, From Passion To Passive Income) mentioned how maintaining a good relationship with colleagues can be of immense assistance to you when starting a business.

I cannot overemphasize how important your network is in the success of your next job or career. Therefore, you need to take stock of those you associate with and be truthful to yourself if they can actually help you in your anticipated journey towards achieving your aim. If not, then start being proactive in building your network and be conscious of it.

I once listened to a recording of Ramit Sethi (Founder of iwillteachyoutoberich.com) where he spoke about how he assisted one of his intern to get a job. This is the power of network.

This is not to say that you will start ignoring those that are not helpful or try to avoid them. No! They might become helpful to you tomorrow. All you want to do is to build a relationship with people that can provide positive personal and professional support to you and vice versa.

I will conclude by telling you that you must also be prepared to provide something of value to those you network with as stated in the opening quote of this chapter; "Your network is your net worth." So you must also show to those you network with that you are a valuable member of their networks' too.

All the jobs I have done up until today and even the business opportunities that have come my way, have all been the product of those I have in my network. Therefore, I charge you to build yours too.

Action: Let's begin the process of hooking you up and helping you build a strong network.

Write down three aspects of your life. Name three people in each aspect and what they contribute to enhancing that particular aspect of your life. Also, write what you contribute to their lives.

Aspects	People	Their Contributions	Your Contributions

Chapter 7

Create a Plan

"If you fail to plan, you will surely plan to fail."
- Anonymous

Dollar for your thought

Have you ever experienced a time when you recorded an outstanding success back to back without any form of planning?

A farmer does not just wake up one day and start harvesting different crops. He must have put in the work (more details in the next chapter on this) beginning from the crop to plant, when to plant, what is required to grow the plant, when to weed, when to apply fertilizer and water the plant, how to tackle pest and predators, until harvest time.

PS: I'm not a farmer. So you can add what I missed out.

The concept is what I need you to focus on. You will agree with me that for the farmer to have a successful planting season and meaningful yield, he must have planned how he would go about planting his crops.

Agreed, there might be (and often times there are) some challenges during the planting season but he would have factored that in during the planning period. And if any unforeseen challenges occur, they might affect his yield at the end of the day. However, if he had planned well, the impact of the challenge would be minimized to a great extent.

This is the method you should adopt in making your next move to quit your job. You must plan how you want to go about leaving your present job and the next steps you need to take when making your next move.

Consider the following questions. Also, feel free to add to the list.

a. Do you want to secure another job before leaving your present employment?

b. Do you want to quit and thereafter begin the process of job search after quitting? If yes, why?

c. Would you require some months off after quitting to go on a holiday and start thinking about your next move or you want to figure out what you want out of life before quitting? If holidaying, where do you intend to visit and why?

d. For (b) and (c), you need to also ask yourself; "Do I have enough savings to live on during this period?" If yes, how much is your savings and do you have a budget for your calculation.

e. Do you have sufficient knowledge of the new role you want to assume or the industry you are switching to or the business you want to start?

f. Do you need to learn a new skill before quitting? What skill is it?

g. How will you acquire the skill?

h. How long would it take to acquire this skill?

i. How much does it cost and how will you finance it?

© Copyright 2017|www.facebook.com/groups/themillennialemployeescorner

You need to do this as swift as possible and do not get caught up in too much planning to the extent that you overanalyze and get paralyzed in the planning stage. Depending on how relevant your goal is for the next move, this should PULL you through this stage quickly so that you can start implementing.

Action: How about adding life to your plans immediately? Your plans will definitely come to life once you perform the below activities. Check them out!

Write responses to the questions in the chapter here. Be totally honest in your responses.

a. _____

b. _____

_____

c. _____

_____

_____

d. _____

_____

_____

e. _____

f. _____

© Copyright 2017|www.facebook.com/groups/themillennialemployeescorner

_____

_____

g. _____

h. _____

i. _____

_____

If you get here, then I believe you must have responded to the questions. Now, that is the first step in adding life to your plans.

Read your responses every day and take a step a day in actualizing what you have written.

Put a timeline to them and begin to put resources aside, be it time or money, in bringing the plan to fruition.

Chapter 8

Practice Your Craft

"Practice does not make perfect. Practice reduces imperfection."
- Toba Beta

Dollar for your thought

Reflect on a time when you carried out a task and you said to yourself; "I could have done it better".

Aristotle said and I quote "For the things we have to learn before we can do them, we learn by doing them".

Isn't he so right?

You have to start doing what you have decided to engage in when you quit your job from now while you are still in your present employment. This is because it will reduce the length of time it would have taken you to get it right when you finally jump ship. And as Toba Beta has said, practice reduces imperfection.

About two years ago, a friend of mine approached me and told me he would like to quit his job. We had several discussions and I discovered that he knew why he wanted to quit and he had a plan. Part of his plan was to start the business he wanted to leave his job for before calling it over with his job.

He did that for three months, made an income equal to his present salary and he turned in his resignation letter.

Hence, if your decision for wanting to quit your job is to start a business and the business will fail, it would have failed or at least you would have seen warning signs early before quitting. This might assist you in making the right decision on when to actually resign so you do not leave too early and start regretting your decision.

Luckily for my friend, the business took off well. Assuming the business did not do well, he won't have resigned his job after three months.

If you want to change your career, you will have the privilege of knowing what it entails or what additional knowledge you need to acquire to make you better suited for the new career that you want to pursue.

Practicing your craft early makes you a perfect fit for your next endeavor. You would have seen your areas of weakness and discover the areas where you need improvement early enough to develop yourself in those areas.

You equally still have access to financial resources- no matter how little - to assist you in improving on those areas. This is better for you rather than quitting and then discovering later that you need to learn some things. It could encroach into your savings; something which you did not plan for. It might also destabilize you or eventually disrupt your plans.

I remember when I quit my first job to start my own business. I thought that my passion and the knowledge I had about my next endeavor would be sufficient to make me successful. Although I knew at that time that the path might be a bit rough but I was also certain that I would make it through.

My dear, I was very wrong.

It turned out that there was a lot more to learn in my newly found industry. The worst thing was that my idea was too early for that industry. It became difficult to get paying clients for my service and even while I offered to render my service for free, not so many wanted to listen. I ran out of cash and I had to change course after a long time trying to figure out how to get paid proved futile. I should have been smart enough to practice my craft before leaving my job. Too bad!

Action: Let's begin the practice process. Look below and get the idea.

If you are switching career;

Identify how you can begin to test your knowledge of the new industry you are switching to. If you can find the time and get somewhere to volunteer within that new industry, that would be great.

If you are transitioning into entrepreneurship;

Write down how you intend to offer your service.

_____
_____
_____
_____
_____

Figure out how to get paid. It is very important. Write it down here.

_____
_____

_____

_____

Determine whom your first three clients would be. Write out how you will go about reaching out to them.

_____

_____

_____

_____

After this, you should be able to identify what works, what doesn't, and how to hone your skill in the process.

BONUS CHAPTERS

Having read this much, it is my belief that you would have learnt a great deal on what you need to do to make that change you desperately want to make. You should have begun the process already, too.

The last three chapters will further assist you to polish your quitting plan. Most likely, it will also serve you well beyond the process of quitting your job.

Chapter 9

Find Your Purpose

"He who has a 'why' to live for can bear almost any 'how.'"

- Friedrich Nietzsche

Finding your purpose can be a daunting task. And I mean it in every sense of the word.

Trust me, I have been there and I am still going through it because it is a continuous journey.

But what you should never be caught doing is not taking steps to begin this process. You have to ensure that you are consciously finding your "why" in life. Pay attention to your inner self. Understand your surroundings. What keeps you on your toes, that is, what makes you unsettled? What frustrates you? What excites you? What fills your thoughts mostly when you catch yourself thinking? These things can nudge you towards finding what you are best suited for in life.

Responses to these questions can equally assist you when you feel the need to quit your job and head for the next thing in your life.

Action: Are you ready to find your purpose?! Then, do these.

Write down your responses to the questions in this chapter.

Do not rush.

Ponder upon them well but don't procrastinate.

Now, start writing;

_____
_____
_____
_____
_____
_____
_____
_____
_____
_____
_____

CHAPTER 10

Build a Deep Pocket

"All days are not same. Save for a rainy day. When you don't work, savings will work for you."
- Anonymous

Experts have continuously advised to save up at least six months' worth of expenses before leaving your job so as to have a sizeable nest egg that allows you focus on finding a new job that fits you perfectly.

This can equally serve as a supplement to your income if you are switching career or starting out with a low salary job. Also, it can serve as "expenses security" for you if your aim is to start a business of your own when you quit.

Action: Do you want to learn how to build a deep pocket? Let me show you how.

Starting from now;

- Start saving up every monetary gift that you receive.

- Save at least 10% of your net monthly income (that is, your income before you start spending it).

- Develop a monthly budget before the beginning of each month and do not spend beyond what you have in your budget for the month.

- Do not spend beyond your income and always avoid borrowing.

Chapter 11

Quit with your head, not your emotions

"Never make a decision to quit with your emotions, do so with your head."
 - Suhaib Arogundade

Quitting is not something you should do impulsively or when you are frustrated. You have to think deeply and understand the real reason behind your decision. If you have not done this, you should do so right now. Also, you must ensure that the decision to leave your job is the right one because you cannot take it back once you quit.

More importantly, you should check to see if the reasons you want to quit are things (whether it is more money, a promotion or a more reasonable workload) that you could resolve by talking somewhat candidly with your boss. By weighing your options, you will be able to confidently proceed with your decision.

Once again, do ensure that you have thoroughly pondered upon the decision before making a leap.

APPENDICES

Knowledge and Skills

How to develop required skills if you lack any;

- Volunteering
- Travelling
- Taking online courses: Examples of online course resources; udemy.com, teachable.com, edx.com
- Attending seminars
- Interning

Networking

- Personal

Family friends, immediate and extended family members, and children's contacts such as parents of their friends or neighbors

- Professional

Current or former employers, colleagues at work, fellow students, academic tutors, professional associations, and the people you meet at training programs or seminars.

- Extracurricular

Exercise groups, social clubs, alumni associations, community associations, and religious associations.

REFERENCES

- Leap Africa Employability Programme Manual
- www.goodreads.com/quotes/tag/practice
- www.quotesgram.com
- https://www.monster.com/career-advice/article/things-to-do-before-quitting-job-you-hate
- http://www.goodnet.org/articles/690

Thank You So Much

I am glad you took out time to read this book to the end.

I hope you have enjoyed the book as much as I loved writing it for you. And I believe this is the beginning of a very interesting interaction between us.

If you have an extra second, I would love to hear what you think about the book.

Please leave a comment on the site where you purchased it.

Also, if you would like me to coach you in your journey to quit or just require a one-on-one clarity session with me, kindly click this link and I will get in touch with you as soon as possible.

PS: If you read the electronic version of this book, kindly do not share or distribute to anyone as I spent tons of hours and effort to put this book together.

If you did all the task in the book, you will know that it is for you to keep as you will need to always make reference to your responses.

Thanks once again, and I wish you nothing less than phenomenal achievement!

Suhaib Arogundade
A learning junkie who trains millennial employees to get the best out of their jobs and live a life of their dreams

© Copyright 2017|www.facebook.com/groups/themillennialemployeescorner

Suhaib Arogundade

About the Author

I am a Civil Engineer and a Right Learning Method (RLM) Advocate. I started working almost immediately after my graduation from the University and quit after 10months to start my own business. After hustling for 2 years with little success and nothing in the bank, I went back to a paid employment. This new employment literarily changed my life. It gave me the fortune of writing this book in a bid to share with you what I wished I had known then before quitting first my job. I have shared some of the principles in this book with friends and it worked for them and I am also practicing the principles myself. I wish you a wonderful reading.

You can shoot me an email at **esarogundade@gmail.com** for a quick chat on how I can be of more help to you or to share how this book has assisted you in your journey of thinking through and making your decision to quit.

For more support, kindly join my Facebook group so that together we can make the quitting journey an effortless one. www.facebook.com/groups/themillennialemployeescorner

You can also click here for a free 15 minutes clarity session with me to explore your decision to quit.

OR click here for your free Self Evaluation Tool

To your Phenomenal Achievement always!

Suhaib AROGUNDADE
Self-Development Propagator|RLM Advocate|Just-In-Time Learning Advocate|Employee Happiness and Safety Coach

© Copyright 2017|www.facebook.com/groups/themillennialemployeescorner

Suhaib Arogundade

Disclaimer

The information contained in this book is my opinion and it is based on my experience, interaction with different categories of employees, and from research.

Results to be derived after reading this book might not be typical. It will depend on the stage you are in your journey as an employee and on the level of development you have attained before reading the book.

Additional Information

For those who might have purchased the hardcopy only, here are the links for the Coaching/One-on-One session and Self Evaluation Tool

Coaching/One-on-One Session:
https://goo.gl/forms/KM7HQeP8DxU7cCrk2

Self Evaluation Tool:
http://bit.ly/2p4fsig

Who am I for you to read this book

I am a schooled Civil Engineer turned a Right Learning Method (RLM) Advocate. I started working almost immediately after graduation from the University and quit after 10months to start up my own business. After hustling for 2 years with little success and nothing in the bank, I went back to paid employment. This new employment literarily changed my life. It was the one that gave me the fortune of writing this book in a bid to share with you what I wished I had known then before jumping ship when I first quit my job. The content of this book would have also been of great help to me when I went in and out of employment during my hustling period. I have shared some of the principles in this book with friends and it worked for them and I am also practicing the principles now myself.

I wish you a wonderful read and you can shoot me an email at esarogundade@gmail.com for a quick chat on how I can be of more help to you or to share how this book has assisted you in your journey of thinking through and making your decision to quit.

To your Phenomenal Achievement always!

Suhaib Arogundade

Self Development Propagator | RLM Advocate | Just-In-Time Learning Advocate

www.ingramcontent.com/pod-product-compliance
Lightning Source LLC
Chambersburg PA
CBHW021445170526
45164CB00001B/401